Copyright (

MW01226591

ISBN : 9798623830562

Library of Congress Control Number: 2018675309
Printed in the United States of America

CONTENTS

INTRODUCTION

Thank you for reading volume 2 and coming on anohter journey with me. all stories written and created are all real and from the authors life and meant to bring comfort and peace and healing until your lives.

CHAPTER 1 CHANGE

◆ ◆ ◆

This story was inspired by one of the reasons I started my books. I realized the changes I was going through, and how important it was for me and why I can write these stories. I truly want to see people happy and becoming their greatest version. A whole other world that gets opened up. I want to help but you have to want the change. I remember me fighting this change I am going through right now. Me fighting it caused a lot of bad situations in my life, but it opened my eyes to the fact that I was not in alignment with my higher nature and my higher calling. We all have a responsibility to do the best we can with our lives. There are no excuses, either you want to live your best life, or you can settle with the cards you were dealt. Change is very scary. I am not going to lie to you and tell you that it's easy... No, you are going to fail, you are going to make mistakes. It has road-blocks with twist and turns and situations that will make you feel like you want to give up. I really hate to see people with gifts and talents that will never be seen or used. I really believe the hard times are necessary. It is sharpening your mind and your skills and how you view yourself. I thought that at certain points I learned the lesson, but in reality, it is an ongoing process. There is always more to learn and tests that will continue to come into your life. Your path is designed for you so follow it and go with the change. I have seen fear stop people from doing what they love or passionate about... and it almost got me too. The fear of the unknown has people trapped. I always wondered where did this fear come from? Why are there so many people afraid of doing something that makes them uncomfortable? We all have a personal reason for why we will not take risk or go for our dreams. Change is very uncomfortable, and it does not end until you get rid of all the things holding you back mentally and physically, but it will help you grow. I heard something somewhere that baby steps still move you forward and anything not growing is dead. Even if you cannot see the final destination yet, you need to have a plan and follow through with it. You have to be smart and work productively. You have to trust yourself and the process and never allow anyone, no matter who they are, to you discourage you or make you feel like you are not good enough. Discipline yourself. Even if you complete one goal or dream, keep going and learning and pushing for more. I remember how scary it was for me. I had to keep telling myself I deserve to be happy and feel fulfilled. I had to start removing negative people, thoughts and things and me saying, no, it can never happen, to yes it can happen. Yes, I can do it. You have to stay positive no matter what is going on in your life and have gratitude. It is very important. There are many things I have done and still doing to become my greatest version. I only seek to share some of my knowledge so if you decide to step into the change it will ease your journey, but you have to want it. If I knew what I know now, I would have taken life head on with a lot more personal power.

CHAPTER 2 KEEP YOUR IMAGINATION AND CREATIVITY

◆ ◆ ◆

Growing up my life was pretty rough, but those lonely days where it was just me and my thoughts, I still kept my imagination and creativity alive. I guess it was my getaway from everything that was going on in my life. Even though I had siblings and we played together, I felt like we didn't connect until we got older. I was the black sheep of my family so I never really fit in. I used to draw and paint and got really good at it. When I got older, it helped me draw and map out how I pictured things in my mind. I loved to play sports. My favorite sport was basketball. I loved the way it feels to play, and I played at least 10 different ones growing up. As I get older, I still play sports, but not as much as I want. But when I do, it still makes me feel free and connects me to myself and other people from all backgrounds while having fun. I even worked on computers and other electronics, just taking them apart and putting it back together and learning the way they worked. It became very useful because a lot of people have to spend money to fix and learn things about electronics, but it's a skill I have kept alive with my creativity and imagination. Now as an adult, it is still fun for me and saves me money and trouble. Music and writing is where my heart is. Growing up, it was my safe haven. I loved singing and writing. It took me to another place with it. I was using my creativity to shoot for the stars and created a better life inside my mind and it stuck with me and kept me pushing as an adult. I didn't understand how good I was at it. I guess the hard times and me always wanting to help people crafted me into what I am doing now. So, to whoever is reading this, keep your imagination and creativity alive no matter how silly it may seem. All the geniuses in the world were very intelligent because of their imagination and their creative weirdness, and them being able to continue to be themselves regardless of how people viewed them. I think as we get older, we forget how important it is.

CHAPTER 3 LOSS

◆ ◆ ◆

Losing someone you love, there is never a right time for it and really no words to describe it. The best thing you can do for yourself and anyone else around you is to heal from it. How you respond to it will shape the inside of you. Don't ever become a victim to loss or grief, it is a part of life. People can take loss in different ways. Some people can't feel it right away because of the state of shock they are in and will make them seem emotionless. Some people feel the loss immediately and cave into the emotions. Either way it goes, you need to let it out. Embrace those emotions and keep your heart clean from bitterness or hatred. We will not always understand why god takes certain people from us, but we have to trust that its apart of a bigger plan. If you are in a bad place or don't know how to overcome the emotions you are feeling, think about it this way... you owe it to yourself to pick yourself up and be the best person you can be. Honor the ones that are no longer here by moving forward and keeping your loved one's memories alive. Use your life to live for them since their time on earth has ended. Losing someone can feel unbearable no matter what relationship or compacity they held in your life. Even situations where that person may still be living but you are no longer speaking... that pain can feel the same. The pain can hit you at any moment. There is no timing for these things.

What I can tell you is that when it hurts, embrace it. Try to understand how you feel and heal from it. Over time it will start to make sense for why the pain needed to be dealt with. The hurt and confusion will lose its power over you... the pain will slowly fade. I promise you will become better and believe that everything will be okay. You will thank yourself later down the road.

CHAPTER 4 DEAR MOTHER

◆ ◆ ◆

I really want to write a letter/story for you, so that I can express what needed to be said a long time ago. Where I am now and where I was a few years ago, it could never be done properly. Now that I have healed internally, I hope my words reach you eventually. I love you and even though my memories of you aren't the best, you are my mother and you brought me into this world, so I feel it is the most respect I deserve to give you. Growing up and being beaten and abused by you, I'm not sure why you did it, but I forgive you. I know you will never admit it, but you trying to take my life was the beginning of me really feeling worthless and internally making me want to take my own life over time. Then there was the time you left us at a family members house, I was molested and you took me to get checked out. Thank got it didn't go any further. I'm guessing that's why you took us from her house. I wanted to save you from the pain of knowing it actually happened because you prided yourself on a few things, but sadly you failed at that one. You doing what you did to me as a child, I was fearful of you which made me fearful of the world. My heart was breaking every day and thank god it never crumbled. I guess you did your best, as far as your heart would allow. But you never healed your own wounds from your childhood and growing up, but I wish the cycle would have ended when you brought me into this world. The questions that I wish I got answers to are why you couldn't be there when I needed you... when I needed to be taught how to be a black women growing up in this world... why, when I was sick I had to learn to give myself medicine... or when I was sad or feeling down I couldn't run to you... or why you dumped so many responsibilities on me as a child? Honestly, nothing in my memory reminds me of why I ever needed you. I am sorry if my words seem harsh, these are just my honest emotions being poured from my heart. It needed to be expressed because my heart does not deserve to hold on to that baggage any longer. Overall, I am grateful for the way my life turned out because everything I needed to become this beautiful woman I am today, that I crafted, and it means more to me. You did keep a roof over my head, clothes on my back and all the materialistic things that I needed or wanted as a child. I just hate that I felt abandoned just to sleep in a warm bed. I want to put so much more into this story, but I feel like I got enough out. My heart is clean, and I forgive you for everything you put me through. It was for me not you. I hope you are doing okay. I know we haven't spoken in a while, but I tried to have a relationship with you even after what you did when my father died. I realized you were going to continue to keep digging that knife deeper and deeper, but I'm over that phase now. If you ever need me I will always be there, but until then, I'm going to end this with I love you and I forgive you. I hope that now my heart is healed internally, that this message reaches you eventually.

CHAPTER 5 COLOR

◆ ◆ ◆

This is a story inspired by me being tired of explaining why I choose to not judge someone by the color of their skin. Truth be told, I love everyone regardless of how you look or how you speak or what you choose to do in your spare time. The color of your skin is very real, I am not saying that I do not see it, but we are human beings first. We all want almost the same things out of life whether it is to not feel pain, hurt, live paycheck to paycheck, to be happy and to feel full filled in this life... the list gives on. I really do not know why God has made me this way, to love everyone, don't hurt anyone, be kind, but to fear no one. God gave me this heart and vision to carry out, so who am I not to listen, above all else he is who I will follow. The way my life has played out is when God tells me to follow a certain moral compass that I need to. If I stray, he will put me back on it and there's a lesson I will have to learn in the process. So, I will ease my journey with not putting up a fight. I do not know why God wants me to share my story or experiences and use the gift he gave me, but It will be revealed eventually. Until then I will continue to spread love, not hate. Spread positivity. Help the next person and still love the people who won't show it back regardless of the color of their skin. I am coming to a point in my life that I can do these things and not hold onto energy of negativity, I can release it. I am still learning who I am and what I was put here for. I am not perfect, but I am becoming my greatest version. Whoever has an issue with my character, I really could care less. This is who I am and if you dislike me for loving everyone and not judging them, it says a lot about your character. Racism and prejudice are very real. I have a lot of stories where I have been judged by the color of my skin. It hurt once upon a time, but I came to the realization that they don't know any better. I am proud of who I am. I love my chocolate skin and my melanin. I must lead by example, I never understood why I always felt that in the pit of my gut. I choose to keep my heart clean from the evil in this world. My heart is pure, but please don't take it as a weakness. God made me in his image and in the process, he built strength, courage, and was teaching me to be fearless so I can carry out his mission and to fear no one that comes along. The moral of this story is to be kind to one another regardless of their skin color. We all have so much we can learn from one another. I get it, this world will try to divide us and keep us in the mental state where we think we are too different, that there is no way we could ever understand each other, but that is not true. We have more in common than you might think. Spark a conversation with some one that doesn't look like you and you will be very surprised about the outcome. Mistreating someone because of what they look like or their views are different from yours is crazy. Think about it... We live in a world that separates each other by skin color, what we believe in and how we choose to live our lives. Which is not how we build a better future with more peace, so there can be more love in the world instead of hate.

CHAPTER 6 BULLY

◆ ◆ ◆

I always felt this story needed to be written. I wanted to own up to my role and express the effects that bullying has on people. I realized no matter how old you are, no matter where you are in life, there are so many people being bullied or someone doing the bullying. Honestly, I want to be forgiven because I should have known better, but sometimes in life you do certain things, and it allows you to change your ways and maybe teach someone in the process. I want to forgive the ones that bullied me too. I'm going to break down both sides as honest as possible. I'm going to start with being a bully. When you are a bully, treating people any way you want, hurting them physically and mentally because you think it's going to make you feel better about what you have going on personally in your life, or makes you look cool. It is just a figment of your imagination. What you are really doing is running from yourself. Most bullies feel like they can gain something from it by hurting someone else. Now does that make sense or sound cool to you? What if the shoe was on the other foot, and you found someone that used you as a punching bag or an emotional dumping ground to deal with their own internal wounds? If you cannot deal with your own emotional trauma and you feel your only option is to hurt someone else, find another way. Seek silence and understand your own emotions and solutions to your problems. There is always another way, trust me. Meditate if you need options or clarity. It's okay to disconnect from the world to do some healing. I learned I was bullying people because I was bullied on top of everything else that was wrong with my life and I was more internally messed up than I thought. I was picking on people I thought was emotionally weaker than I was, but in reality, I was the weak one crumbling from the pain that kept me feeling down. In some sick way I started to believe they deserved it, or I was helping them in some way. Helping them build courage when in reality, I was a coward, running from the demons in my heart. Even though I was young when I was a bully, part of me knew it was wrong, but I did it anyway. I'm going to speak to the ones who may be getting bullied and tell you about how it was for me and what I took from it. I know being bullied can make you feel like you are less than who you are, but you are not worthless. You are strong and brave. Honestly, I'm not saying being bullied should be tolerated in no shape or form, but if you are going through it learn from it. Speak up regardless of if you are afraid or not. Stand up for yourself and don't let anyone use you for their own self gain, no matter what the circumstances are or who they are. If you are being bullied don't stoop to their level, be smart... trust me, if you stand up for yourself, they will stop. Bullies are looking for the love and attention they are not getting. Don't become bitter or filled with self-hatred and don't allow yourself to feel like you don't want to live or cause you to think about hurting yourself or others. I know how far it goes down that rabbit hole, don't do it and it's not your fault. Once you understand the mind of a bully, they will lose their power over you so use that and rise above it. I am going to end this with a short and sweet message for both sides. In some way, the message is one in the same because both of you have become victims to what this life will do to you internally. Do not give up and don't think you're a bad person or deserve what you are going through. Stand tall and deal with what's going on. It's a bigger world out here. Stop hurting yourself. Don't think hiding or running from your problems will make it go away because it won't. Find a better outlet, a hobby or passion. Help one another and grown into something better. Life will be easier when we all stop running from what's wrong.

CHAPTER 7
COMPASSION PT. 2

◆ ◆ ◆

This is a story about how I paid it forward for the next person. There was a man that came into my job I worked at and I could tell everything was off with him mentally, physically, spiritually and emotionally. I could see he was drained from the inside out. His legs were wobbling as he tried to walk towards me, like the world and all its crap got dumped on his shoulders. I immediately felt so bad for him. As he came up to me to make a purchase he could barely speak, tears were coming from his eyes and snot was coming from his nose. On the contrary, he was a good looking, well put together man. I could tell on a normal day he was not this bent out of shape. So, he began to speak and most of the words couldn't be understood, he apologized for not being able to fully get it out, I told him it's okay and I asked him what was wrong. He tried to mutter out the words, but I stopped him. My heart was breaking seeing the tears and snot running down his face. I offered him a tissue and he gladly accepted it and then he continued to speak. He said he had some court stuff going on and from the looks of it his emotions meant he could be facing time in jail or prison. He said all he had was his P.O. (probation officer) in his life right now keeping him sane. He said, "I try to do my best and be the best person I can, but I don't know." and he paused for a second, put his head down and I could see the tears form back in his eyes. After listening for a little while, I see that he was done speaking. So, I began to speak, but the moment I did I could feel all those moments and what it made me feel in those times, when I only wanted to be a better person and just be happy and live my life freely. I had to compose myself because if I did not, I would not of have been able to relay my message to him. I told him I understand I have been there, where all my efforts felt like they were going in vain. I said I had to pass those tests and stay positive through it all and that everything was going to be okay, trust me. Don't stop believing and trying to do the best you can. He listened closely and I could tell I had his full attention because there was no more tears just pure attention. After I was done speaking, he said thank you, as his lips still trembled from all the emotions, he was feeling a little better. I told him your welcome and I smiled. It warmed my heart and after he left that night, I prayed he would not give up and that he would pass those tests. The moral of this story is, that in life you must be strong and overcome hardships, solve your problems and evolve and grow especially if you genuinely want what you deserve. You can't give up and you have to respond accordingly, still have gratitude in the forefront because only then can you make the right choices. Pay it forward, show compassion and kindness. Who knows, you could be saving a life.

CHAPTER 8 MY FURRY FRIEND

◆ ◆ ◆

This is a story for the ones that has had to deal with the loss of a pet/friend. It took me over a year to even get to a point where I could write this. Even though my heart still hurts from it, I am going to release my emotions into every word I am writing. My dogs name was 50 Cal, aka Cal. I had him for 5 ½ years. He was a beautiful Pit Bull with white and brown fur and hazel eyes that changed colors in the sunlight. The day I got him from his litter he was about 3 months old. I was not even going to pick him at first. I wanted a different one because he was not like the other pups, he was a loner pup. I ended up getting him anyway. It turned out a year later, 50 Cal would be the last one to survive. All the other ones died from an illness. The day I took him home he was already attached to me. I had pets in the past, but none of them connected to me so quickly. On the way to bringing him to see his new home he was a little scared, but he wanted to sit behind my back while I was driving. I allowed it for a little while because I knew he had never been on a car ride, let alone a long one from Nc to Va. Over time even when I'm not driving, before he got too big, he would continue to want to do that. When I got home, he was opening up a little more. He was following my feet as I walked around the house and even when I would go to class, he would lay on my side of the bed right after I left. It was like he missed me, and I only found out he was doing that because one day I forgot my books for class, so I turned around and there he was, just relaxing. Cal knew my moods and he got me through some of the toughest times. Honestly, he eased the pain by showing me love and he never let me sit in my sorrows. It was like he could feel something was off, like a sixth sense. I remember how he wanted to play. He would take something I had near me, walk away with it and look back at me like are you going to come get it. When I would say give it back and motion like I was going to get up, he would get in a stance like he was going to take off the moment I got up. As soon as I got up, he ran and I would chase him until I finally caught him. After that, he was like okay now that you're up its time to play because then he started to chase me, and I would be running around and rolling in laughter. It became a regular thing after the first time. There are so many stories I could tell where he filled my heart with joy, but I want to get to the real reason I am writing this story. As the time went by, I started to realize something did not seem right with him. Even though he was still full of energy, he would act normal up until certain times of the day, then he would act strange. Even when I would say, "50 Cal what is wrong?", all he would do is walk over to me and lick my face. The only time Cal normally would not be his full energetic self is when I used to take him hiking with me. He would be tired after and want to go to sleep after we got home which was normal because I would do the same. I could feel it in my gut something was off, so the day I seen his stomach swell up, I looked it up because I knew that was not okay. Everything I read was saying it could be life or death kind of situation. Little did I know when I took him to the vet, I would be preparing to say my final goodbye. The day I took him to the vet, I honestly had no idea what to expect as we waited to be seen. When it was time to go to the back room, I noticed a box of tissue on the counter I thought it could be a sign but shrugged it off because it was the last thing I wanted to think about. Someone finally came in to ask questions before the doctor came in. When they finally checked Cal out, we talked for a little while. The Vet wanted to run some tests on him so we could have a better understanding of what we were dealing with. I could hear Cal in the back making noises and it bothered me, but I was just hoping that whatever was causing discomfort was not that bad. The doctor brought him back to me and 50 Cal was still running around and being noisy and the doctor told me that 50 Cal had cancer and was bleeding from his stomach... I asked what can I do? And what procedures do you have? He said they do have procedures, but for Cals case there was not a good chance he would survive even after the procedure was done. I was in shock because the doctor asked me am I understanding what he was telling me. It was like his words were floating in the air and they did not connect with my ears or brain yet. That is when Cal stopped snooping around the room and sat beneath my legs in front of me and put his head back and looked me in my eyes. My eyes connected with his and it was like time stopped and it was just me and him in that moment. I forgot we were even in the vet office or that I just received the worst news of my life. I do not know how long we were even staring into each other's eyes, but once Cal looked back forward at the doctor, it was like he sent a signal to me to pay attention to what the doctor was telling me. Once I started to speak again, all my emotions poured out and the tears started to flow. The doctor left out the room after we talked for a little. We begin wrapping things up with my options and what I may have to do next. I could tell all the people coming in the room to ask me questions before I left could feel my pain. When it was time to leave, I stood up, and it was like some movies where someone will get bad news and everyone around them is moving in slow motion or the noise around them was muffled. That is exactly how I felt. I thought I was going to lose my balance trying to reach for Cal's leash, but I did not. I could see the doctor making sure I did not. I went home with Cal and could not stop crying. I could not even go to work for a few says on top of me having to figure out when was going to have to put him down. My heart was breaking, my best friend that always showed me loyalty and even when I wasn't being the nicest, he still showed me kindness. When that day came it was a pain in my heart I carried around for months. It has been almost 2 years now since I lost him, but I had to learn the lesson from it. Cal taught me how to love someone, even if they have 4 legs or a tail and looked nothing like me. Cal also taught me that when life is rough, to still see the beauty beyond just what you feel in that moment. Some much more lessons in the mist of darkness. I don't think I could truly find another friend like him even though he was a dog. He was more trustworthy than anyone I know. Damn, writing this story I thought it would be easier, but it just reminds me that you are no longer here, and I miss you buddy. I know I will always keep your memories alive and I will live my best life and I hope you are having a good time up and doggie heaven. You were my little angel, I guess it was your time.

CHAPTER 9 PAINFULLY BEAUTIFUL

◆ ◆ ◆

Life is painfully beautiful. When I look at where I was and where I am now, is some kind of wonderful. Through the tears and the painful nights, I cried thinking what a life, something happens, and a thought runs through my mind saying, "Dear child don't cry, I have always been keeping you aware of the life I have been creating for you." Through the pain will you only know true pleasure. Through the sadness will you only be able to maneuver through the weather. It is not to keep you feeling down, I am trying to show you how powerful you are, so don't cry. You are strong. I created this painfully beautiful life to show you how worthy you are.

CHAPTER 10
SUICIDE

◆ ◆ ◆

I really wanted to write about suicide, but I could not find the right words. So, I took my time to think about it for a while, so when I write you feel my words. You are going to be okay no matter what you are going through. Do not give up because you are being here, means a lot. I may not know you, but I love you. You may not believe in yourself, but I believe in you. You are special because god made you. Life is going to be hard and you may feel like there is no way out. I was there at one point where I wanted to be rid of all the pain, heartache and confusion, but little did I know my story would help so many. If I would have given up, I would not be able to tell my story and do what I am doing now. Living here on earth felt like a nightmare where I just wanted to wake up and it felt like that almost every day like nothing was going right. I have felt so much pain it was excruciating many days and many nights... when I was young and even as an adult. Those suicidal thoughts stayed with me up until the age of 23 and I am 28 now. I told myself, if my younger self from the age of 5 or 6 did not give up how dare you even try to. Pass those tests and become a better you. I am sure you have so many gifts and talents you have yet to discover that the world would truly thank you. I do not know if whoever is reading this now will feel my words but do not ever give up. This road on your journey is going to be bumpy, but the world needs you. It's okay to cry sometimes, but do not feel like it is the end of the world. Those hard times, I promise you, builds strength and character... you just have to hold on a little longer. I am still on my journey and I would love to believe it is going to be smooth sailing from here, but I know that in doing what I love it is so worth it. I am getting closer to the life I want every day because I will not give up. If I did, all those times I laid up at night thinking of a better day or even about the horrible times, would all be for nothing. I choose to smile and keep my spirits high. I heard this saying somewhere that the universe is testing you to see what you are made of. I guess if you want something bad enough it wants to see if you have what it takes before it gives it to you. You have made it this far; don't you want to give yourself a real chance to truly live and be the author of your own story? I had to get out of my own way because there is and was nothing holding me back but myself. Heal those wounds and traumas and learn your truth and why you must go through whatever is hurting you. "You are stronger than you think", people would always say to me, but I couldn't understand it... I finally did when it was time for me too. Self-medicating to numb your pain is temporary. Feel those pains. That is the only way to deal with it and heal from it. You cannot run from your problems. No matter how long you try to bury them, they will resurface, and they will play a role in everything you do or think. When I prayed to God I would think, if I did this, why would it really matter? I tried to convince myself that it would be easier if I weren't here anymore. I would say all kinds of things so that what I wanted to do would be easier, but I switched it up. I started to pray to God to help ease the pain and help me find a way to remove these things in my life that only brought me heartache and misery. I believe God wanted to bring me closer, so I knew that he was always there for me. I began praying before I even knew what it really was. My younger self from the age of 5 or 6 knew there was something else out there or someone else out there and so much more to life. So, I took life head on... and if I could do it you can too.

CHAPTER 11
STRONG

◆ ◆ ◆

This is a story about when you are strong. Sometimes you don't know who you can run to because you spend so much time being that shoulder to cry on or that person people run to when they need to heal or get comfort. There are so many times when someone that is so strong, with so much strength, still needs someone to go to or talk to. It's so hard because you are so used to figuring things out on your own and you feel like no one could truly understand what's wrong. So, you keep it to yourself and try to handle it, but suppression leads to depression. Sometimes, all there is to do is cry and break down when there is no one else around. In this life it can be extremely hard, but in choosing to be strong you have to keep your head up and turn to God. I've learned if I don't have any one to talk to, in order to feel comfort or peace I need, I turn to God. He is the only one that will ever truly ease your pain and give you clarity and understanding that you need. I was blessed to have a handful I people in my life, that could understand to a certain extent, but those times end when you are growing and evolving faster than the people around you. My passion for writing is my therapy. Honestly, I do not know what I would be doing without it. I feel free and it keeps me grounded when things are not going to plan. I can express myself and I realized it was a part of my purpose. I thank God for this gift. Somehow, he knew I would find it and use it as my therapy. I am grateful that I can share it with so many. The moral of this story is that even the strongest of the strongest people still need something or someone. Make sure you turn to God or find your passion because it may be a part of your purpose, your gift and your therapy. Please be sure to share it.

CHAPTER 12
DIFFICULT PEOPLE

◆ ◆ ◆

This is about dealing with difficult people. In life I realized how important it is to know how to handle yourself. I want to paint a picture, really tell a story so that you can understand what I am saying. When difficult people act out of character or cause a scene or even be rude for no reason, it has nothing to do with you. It has everything to do with them and what they are going through. I had to watch how I reacted and started to respond accordingly. The moment you react to difficult people you open yourself up and your energy field to everything they had in their energy or in their spirits, to latch on to you and disrupt your energy. Which in turn, will cause you to ruin your day or the part of the day because you have now literally given your energy and power away. When you respond, you're normally able to think before you do anything. It gives you a chance to weigh your options out and listen to that voice of reason. Don't allow people to come into your world and disrupt it. Find a way to shake off the negative energy they give off and remember that what they are upset about or angry about is not your energy it is theirs. Be kind still and keep your composure. They will end up looking like the fool in the end. You will in turn, allow yourself to grow and become better. Overtime, difficult people will lose their power.

CHAPTER 13
WALKING BY FAITH

◆ ◆ ◆

This story is dedicated to anyone that has been walking along their paths, with no idea how you remain strong through it all. When life seemed to be closing in on me, I still continued to break through. My intuition was my guide. I think I was not fully aware of it until I got older. The changes I have been going through has been pushing me into my greatness, and now that my eyes are open there is not stopping it. I don't know where this journey is going to lead me, but I am walking by faith, not sight... a lot of people may not know what that means. When you walk by faith, not sight, you do not know the destination, nor can you see it. Your road map is your faith, and your faith is stronger than anything else because you have an inner power and an inner strength, that will allow you to grow and overlook anything that tries to stop you from reaching the life you want. When you walk by faith, not sight, every day you are building and walking into the unknown. You are allowing your faith to get you through and help you see. I decided to trust the path I was set upon, even if I have no idea where I'm going. I just know the life I deserve and my mission in life. So, I will continue to walk by faith, not sight, and get to my final destination without fear of the unknown stopping me. So, there is no other way to go except up... so, I will see you at the top!

CHAPTER 14
THE SEARCH

◆ ◆ ◆

This maybe one of the most important stories for me that I have written. My transformation was a journey and it dawned on me that I was on the search for a better understanding. All the work I have been putting in, I finally think I found the missing piece. I've asked God many nights to help me along my journey and answer the questions I could not find on my own. My questions were, what would I need to do in order to really take my life to the next level? What will it really feel like to focus on myself instead of everything that distracts me? In reality, I believe I always knew the answers to these questions, I just needed God to open my eyes to it. Circumstances in my life pushed me to the answers I was seeking, one day it hit me that my mission was to find myself first, I needed to understand who I am! When that came to me, it was another needed layer removed. I could finally see that it was always about me. My soul was calling me to reveal itself to the world and to find its place in the universe. I am grateful to the knowledge and I know I was running from myself all this time, but not anymore. I was like a caged lion that wanted to burst out and run in the wild again and claim my rightful place. I was allowing this world to rob me of my senses of me finding myself, but I am ready to embrace it. I know it's going to be a bumpy ride... so, I'll put my seat belt on tight because I won't allow myself to fall off.

AFTERWORD

THANK YOU FOR READING VOLUME 2. I AM VERY GRATE-
FUL YO EVERY ONE THAT PURCHASED A COPY . YOU ARE
ALLOWING ME TO BRING MY DREAMS AND MY GIFTS TO
LIFE. THERE WILL BE MORE BOOKS TO COME FOLLOWNG
THIS ONE.

Follow me on instagram@master_pieces_llc
Follow me on facebook/master pieces llc

ACKNOWLEDGEMENT

Thank you Unique Carter for doing my make up for my authors photo i wish you nothing but the best.
facebook.com/unique makeup

BOOKS BY THIS AUTHOR

Journey To Love And Truth For The Soul Volume 1

This a mini series meant to help you understand trauma and how you can heal from it and become better from it.

Transformation Guide

This is a self help transformation guide, you will be able to write in this book and heal all of your most deepest traumas and track your journey and your transformation along the way.

Made in the USA
Middletown, DE
09 July 2021